S0-BXW-131

The Spanish Missions of Texas

MEGAN GENDELL

Children's Press®
An Imprint of Scholastic Inc.
New York Toronto London Auckland Sydney
Mexico City New Delhi Hong Kong
Danbury, Connecticut

Content Consultant
Donald E. Chipman
Emeritus Professor of History
University of North Texas
Denton, Texas

Library of Congress Cataloging-in-Publication Data

Gendell, Megan.
  The Spanish missions of Texas / by Megan Gendell.
    p. cm.—(A true book)
  Includes bibliographical references and index.
  ISBN-13: 978-0-531-20580-8 (lib. bdg.)   978-0-531-21243-1 (pbk.)
  ISBN-10: 0-531-20580-0 (lib. bdg.)   0-531-21243-2 (pbk.)

1. Missions, Spanish—Texas—History—Juvenile literature.
2. Texas—History—To 1846—Juvenile literature. 3. Indians of North
America—Missions—Texas—Juvenile literature. 4. Indians, Treatment
Of—Texas—History—Juvenile literature. 5. Franciscans—Missions—
Texas—History—Juvenile literature. I. Title. II. Series.

  F389.G46 2010
  976.4'02—dc22   2009016716

All rights reserved. Published in 2010 by Children's Press, an imprint of Scholastic Inc.
Published simultaneously in Canada. Printed in China.
SCHOLASTIC, CHILDREN'S PRESS, A TRUE BOOK, and associated logos are trademarks and/or registered trademarks of Scholastic Inc.

2 3 4 5 6 7 8 9 10 R 19 18 17 16 15 14 13 12 11 10   62

Find the Truth!

Everything you are about to read is true *except* for one of the sentences on this page.

Which one is **TRUE**?

T or F   Texas missions got all of their supplies from Mexico.

T or F   Missionaries brought the first cattle to Texas.

Find the answers in this book.

Contents

THE **BIG** TRUTH!

The Lost Mission of Texas

How did historians learn about a mission
that had disappeared? 26

Mission
San Juan

The Rose Window at Mission San José, is about 7 feet tall.

A canal at Mission San Francisco de la Espada

Priests lead a religious service at a mission in San Antonio.

CHAPTER 1

Heading to Texas

Between 1632 and 1793, Spanish priests traveled north from Mexico and built dozens of missions on land in what is now Texas. Missions were small villages that were started in areas that were home to Native Americans. The priests wanted to **convert** Native Americans to Christianity and their ways of life. The priests were the first European people to settle in Texas.

More than 300 people lived and worked at some Texas missions.

The Spanish government sent explorers from Mexico and Spain to what is now Texas.

European Powers

Since the 1500s, Spain had ruled Mexico. By the 1600s, the Spanish wanted more land to control. They were also looking for gold and other **natural resources**. They set their sights to the north of Mexico and moved into Texas and other parts of what is now the southwestern United States. At this time, both England and France also wanted to control land in North America. Spain believed missions would allow them to dominate the Southwest.

Missionary Men

When the Spanish arrived in Texas, many Native Americans lived there. Both soldiers and religious men called missionaries, or **padres** (PAH-drayz), were sent by Spain to start missions. The padres belonged to a Catholic group called Franciscans (fran-SISS-kunz). At the missions, the padres tried to convert Native Americans to Christianity.

Franciscan priests owned nothing. Even their clothes belonged to the church.

CHAPTER 2

Getting Started

Spain set up 35 missions throughout Texas, but they were not all active at the same time. Finding just the right location was important to the success of a mission. Missions needed to be close to where Native Americans lived so that Native people would come to them. Building near rivers, such as the San Antonio, was also important so there would be water for mission farms.

The Spanish and Native Americans built canals to carry water from the San Antonio River to mission fields.

Inside a Mission

A typical mission included a church, housing for the padres and Native Americans, and workshops for cooking, grinding grain, and making clothes, soap, and other goods. Missions also had farmland and fields where cows, horses, sheep,

and other animals grazed. The farms provided food for the people who lived at the missions. The Spanish also built **presidios** (preh-SEE-dee-ohz), or forts, near missions for protection.

At Mission San José in San Antonio, people used this mill to grind wheat into flour.

Behind Presidio Walls

Presidios included a chapel and living areas for soldiers. Soldiers grew lonely living far from their families, and many ran away. La Bahía (bah-EE-uh), which still stands today in Goliad, Texas, was a typical presidio. At the corners of its thick walls were **bastions** (BAS-chunz), high spots where soldiers stood to fire guns. Like other Texas presidios, La Bahía remained active even after its nearby mission, Mission La Bahia, closed down.

Presidio La Bahía is the oldest standing fort west of the Mississippi River.

Making Connections

The padres urged Native Americans to live at the missions so they could teach them. They tried to convince Native Americans they were friendly by offering them food, water, and gifts. Eventually, hundreds of Native Americans lived and worked at some missions. At others, Native peoples visited but never lived in the missions.

New Ways

At the missions, the padres showed Native Americans how to grow new crops. Native peoples also hunted small animals and gathered plants for food—just as they had done before the Europeans took over the land. Some Native Americans refused to give up their traditional ways. They stayed away from the missions.

Texas Missions

New Mexico

DALLAS

AUSTIN

HOUSTON

SAN ANTONIO

Mexico

Gulf of Mexico

1. San Clemente
2. Corpus Christi de la Isleta del Sur
3. Nuestra Señora de la Limpia Concepción del Socorro
4. San Antonio de Senecú
5. La Navidad en las Cruces
6. El Apóstol Santiago
7. San Francisco de los Tejas
8. Santísimo Nombre de María
9. San Cristóbal
10. Santa María de la Redonda de los Cíbolos
11. San Francisco de los Neches
12. Nuestra Señora de la Guadalupe de los Nacogdoches

13. Nuestra Señora de la Purísima Concepción de los Hasinai
14. San José de los Nazonis
15. Nuestra Señora de Dolores de los Ais
16. San Antonio de Valero
17. San José y San Miguel de Aguayo
18. Nuestra Señora de la Bahía del Espíritu Santo de Zúñiga
19. San Francisco Xavier de Nájera
20. Three East Texas Missions
21. Nuestra Señora de la Purísima Concepción de Acuña
22. San Juan Capistrano
23. San Franciso de la Espada

24. Nuestra Señora de los Dolores del Río de San Xavier
25. San Franciso Xavier de Horcasitas
26. San Ildefonso
27. Nuestra Señora de la Candelaria
28. Nuestra Señora del Rosario
29. San Xavier
30. San Francisco Xavier on Guadalupe
31. Nuestra Señora de la Luz del Orcoquisac
32. Santa Cruz de San Sabá
33. San Lorenzo de la Santa Cruz
34. Nuestra Señora de la Candelaria del Cañón
35. Nuestra Señora del Refugio

15

Native peoples in Texas hunted small animals for food and clothing.

CHAPTER 3

Mission Life

Many of the Texas missions were far from Spanish settlements in Mexico, where supplies and food were plentiful. Because of this, padres started mission farms to provide food. People living at the missions also had to make nearly everything they needed. Native Americans did most of this work for no pay. The padres gave them very little help.

Rabbits were an important food for Native Americans in Texas.

There were no horses in Texas until the Spanish brought them.

Work Days

At the missions, Native American men and boys planted and harvested fields, growing corn, beans, cotton, and other crops. Men also learned to ride horses and herd cattle. Women spun cotton and wool into thread and yarn. They wove fabric and made clothing for everyone at the mission. Women also cooked meals and cared for children.

Building the Missions

The padres and the Native Americans worked together to construct mission buildings. In East Texas, they built missions from pine trees. Other areas of Texas had few trees. In these areas, the Native Americans made bricks out of **adobe** (uh-DOH-bee), a mud mixture that is baked in the sun.

People all over the world have made buildings from adobe.

Strict Schedules

The padres followed a strict schedule every day, and they forced Native Americans to do the same. But Native Americans already had their own schedules and ways of life. Many Native Americans refused to be controlled by the Spanish and ran away from the missions. Sometimes soldiers tracked them down and brought them back to the missions. Once back at the missions, Native people would be punished for having left.

Mission bells were rung to call everyone together for prayers and meals. The bells could be heard for miles around.

Mission San Francisco de la Espada (es-PAH-dah) was first built in East Texas and was later moved to what is now the city of San Antonio.

On the Move

Even after a mission had been open for awhile, it sometimes had to be moved. Missions might be moved halfway across Texas or only a few miles away. Some missions moved closer to good farmland, while others moved to escape the many mosquitoes that carried disease. Many missions had to be rebuilt after floods destroyed them.

A Spanish mission near the Rio Grande, a river in Texas

CHAPTER 4

Missions Across Texas

The first Texas missions were settled in West Texas by padres who had left Mexico to work in New Mexico. Spain built another group of missions in East Texas to gain control of more land there. The missions that lasted the longest were those built along the San Antonio River in central Texas. This was an area where many Native Americans hunted, allowing the padres to reach them easily.

Native Americans in East Texas used the word *tejas* (TAY-has) to mean "friend." This word became the name "Texas."

The First Texas Missions

San Clemente (SAN kleh-MEN-teh), the first Texas mission, was built in 1632 in central Texas. The next Texas mission was not built until 1682. Native people had attacked missions in New Mexico in 1680. They were tired of being mistreated by the Spanish. Hundreds of Spanish people escaped from New Mexico and settled near El Paso, Texas,

where they built Mission Corpus Christi de la Isleta del Sur (KOR-pus KREES-tee DEH LA ees-LEH-tuh DEL SOOR).

Mission Corpus Christi de la Isleta del Sur was destroyed by floods and rebuilt twice.

Mission San Francisco de los Tejas (TAY-hoss) was first built in East Texas in 1690.

Most East Texas missions were made of wood, because they were near pine forests.

Settling East Texas

In 1690, the Spanish began founding missions in East Texas. A few Native Americans in East Texas converted to Christianity. But when an outbreak of disease swept through the area, some Native peoples blamed their new religion and returned to their traditions. Later, many East Texas missions moved to what is now the city of San Antonio.

Everyday objects such as nails, buttons, and beads, have been found in the ruins of San Sabá. This is a decoration that was once used on a sack of flour.

This gold-plated sundial made in 1580 was found at the San Sabá site. A soldier would have carried it in his pocket and used it to help tell time.

Archaeologists have uncovered these stones that people once walked on at San Sabá.

26

The Lost Mission of Texas

Mission Santa Cruz de San Sabá was built in 1757. Only one year later, after an attack by Native Americans, the Spanish abandoned the mission. Its remains were thought to be lost forever. Then, in 1993, a group of historians and archaeologists (ar-kee-AH-luh-jists) who had been looking for San Sabá discovered dozens of pieces of pottery from the mission. And that was just the beginning of what they would find!

27

Presidio La Bahía

The mission and presidio at La Bahía was built in 1722 on the Gulf of Mexico. The local Karankawa (kayr-ahn-KAH-wa) people were not willing to convert to Christianity or follow Spanish ways. So in 1726, La Bahía was moved inland, where different groups of Native people lived. It was moved again in 1749, and it now makes up the heart of the city of Goliad, Texas.

Another mission, Nuestra Señora del Refugio (NWES-truh seh-NYOR-uh DEL re-FU-hyo), was built nearby in 1793. It was the last mission founded in Texas.

Even though La Bahía means "the bay" in Spanish, today it actually stands about 40 mi. (65 km) away from the Gulf of Mexico.

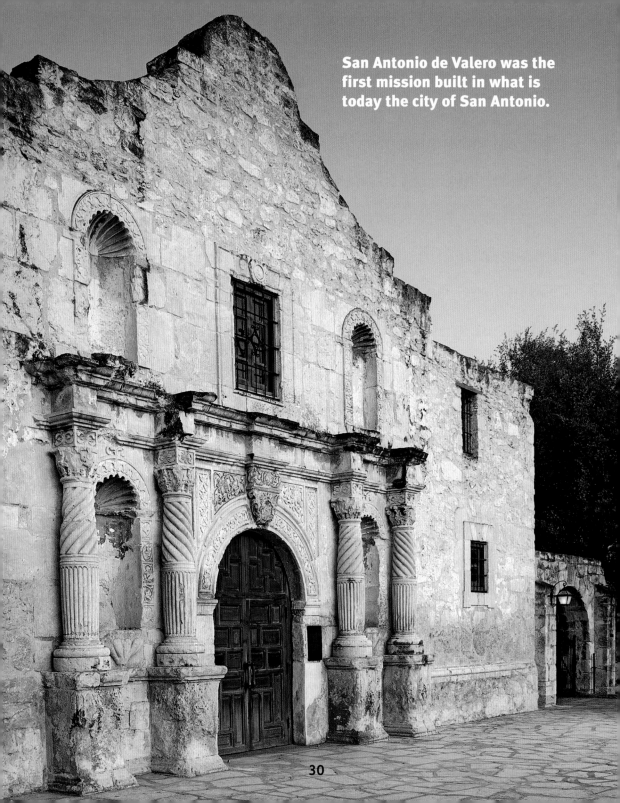

San Antonio de Valero was the first mission built in what is today the city of San Antonio.

CHAPTER 5

The Missions of San Antonio

Along the San Antonio River, the Spanish built five missions considered to be the most successful in all of Texas. They did well for many reasons. These missions were close to Mexico, so they could get supplies more easily than more out-of-the-way missions. They were also near a good source of water that was needed for farming. These missions grew to become large, busy settlements.

The trail of missions along the San Antonio River is 8 mi. (13 km) long.

Mission San Antonio de Valero

Mission San Antonio de Valero was built in 1718 and later became known as the Alamo. A famous battle took place there in 1836. By that time, Mexico was no longer under Spain's control, and Texas was fighting to become independent from Mexico. Hundreds of Texans died fighting for independence in the battle at the Alamo.

"Remember the Alamo" became a battle cry to encourage the Texas army to be brave.

Alamo is the Spanish word for "cottonwood," a kind of tree.

Mission San José

In 1720, Father Antonio Margil (MAR-hil) founded Mission San José near Mission San Antonio. Native Americans at the mission were taught Spanish songs and dances. They learned how to play instruments such as harps, violins, and guitars. San José is

The Rose Window at Mission San José

known for the Rose Window, which features detailed carvings. The window was probably named for the first saint in South America, Saint Rosa of Lima.

Antonio Margil

Father Antonio Margil helped found several missions in Texas, including two in East Texas. After these missions were abandoned in 1719, Father Margil founded Mission San José. He also helped start a school for missionaries in Mexico. Father

Father Margil worked as a missionary in Central America, Mexico, and Texas.

Margil lived a very disciplined life. He traveled only by walking, wore no shoes, and carried no food. It is said that he ate once a day and slept only three hours a night.

Mission Concepción

The first two San Antonio missions were so successful that padres built three more missions nearby, including Mission Concepción (kon-sep-see-OHN). Concepción's church has barely changed since it was first built. Paintings in other missions were destroyed, but the pictures that

padres and Native Americans painted on the walls of Mission Concepción are still visible. At one time, colorful paintings also covered the front of Mission Concepción.

The wall paintings at Mission Concepción include religious symbols and flowers.

Mission San Juan

Mission San Juan was moved from East Texas to the San Antonio River in 1731. Its stone church was completed about 20 years later. Native Americans at San Juan became skilled at growing melons, grapes, and other fruits on its farm. Its ranch had thousands of sheep and cattle. The farm and ranch were so successful that the mission traded extra food with people in Mexico and other places outside of Texas.

In 1762, Mission San Juan owned 1,000 cattle and 3,500 sheep and goats.

The acequia at Mission San Francisco de la Espada was 15 mi. (24 km) long.

Padres sometimes traveled down the acequia in small boats.

Mission San Francisco de la Espada

Native Americans and padres built a system to bring water from the San Antonio River to Mission San Francisco de la Espada and its farmland. The system, known as an **acequia** (ah-SEH-kee-uh), was made up of a series of canals. Today, area farms still use the very same acequia to get water to their fields.

A cowhand tends a herd of horses.

CHAPTER 6

The End of the Missions

By the 1790s, the missions in Texas were struggling. Most Native Americans who lived at the missions had died from diseases brought by the Spanish. Their **population** was almost wiped out. Many missions ended up being abandoned. Later, between 1824 and 1830, the Mexican government closed the missions. But Mexicans continued to travel to Texas with hopes of starting their own ranches and farms on abandoned mission land.

Missions Today

Today, four of the five San Antonio missions are still active churches. The Alamo is now a museum. A few other missions in Texas have been rebuilt or restored, but most of the Texas missions have fallen into ruin. Signs mark the locations of some of the missions, while the exact locations of others remain a mystery.

Timeline of the Texas Missions

1680
Spanish fleeing New Mexico found Mission Corpus Christi de la Isleta del Sur.

1720
Father Antonio Margil founds Mission San José, the largest Texas mission

Digging Up the Past

Archaeologists continue to learn a lot from the ruins of Texas missions and presidios. They have dug up beads, buttons, and pottery at San Sabá and other sites. By doing this, archaeologists can piece together what life was like for the people who wore and used these items hundreds of years ago.

Archaeology students search for items at the Alamo.

1793
Mission Nuestra Señora del Refugio, the last Texas mission, is founded.

1824–1830
The Mexican government shuts down the missions.

Lasting Changes

The missions' lasting influence in Texas can be seen in the Spanish names of the state's cities and rivers. The missions also introduced European fruits and vegetables, as well as cattle and horses, to Texas. These crops and animals proved important to the growth of business in the state. ★

Rio Grande means "big river" in Spanish.

The Rio Grande marks the southern border of Texas.

First mission founded in Texas: Mission San Clemente, in 1632

Last mission founded in Texas: Mission Nuestra Señora del Refugio, in 1793

Number of Spanish missionaries who came to Texas: Nearly 200

Oldest original stone church in the United States: The church at Mission Concepción

Food grown on Texas missions: Corn, beans, potatoes, melons, pumpkins, squash, grapes, and peppers

Animals at Texas missions: Horses, cattle, sheep, goats, and mules

Did you find the truth?

F Texas missions got all of their supplies from Mexico.

T Missionaries brought the first cattle to Texas.

Resources

Books

Asherman, Robyn, and Marina Rizo-Patron. *I Lived in Texas Before It Was Texas: A Child's Life at Mission Espada, San Antonio, Texas, 1762*. Wapiti, WY: Missions and Forts Press, 2004.

Bial, Raymond. *Missions and Presidios*. New York: Children's Press, 2004.

Ditchfield, Christin. *Spanish Missions*. New York: Children's Press, 2006.

Maruca, Mary. *A Kid's Guide to Exploring San Antonio Missions National Historical Park*. Tucson, AZ: Southwest Parks and Monuments Association, 2000.

Teitelbaum, Michael. *Texas, 1527–1836*. Washington, D.C.: National Geographic, 2005.

Wade, Mary Dodson. *Texas Native Peoples*. Chicago: Heinemann, 2008.

Organizations and Web Sites

National Park Service: San Antonio Missions National Historical Park

www.nps.gov/saan/

Discover even more about the history of the San Antonio missions at this site.

Presidio La Bahía

www.presidiolabahia.org

Read more about the long history of La Bahía and see pictures from before it was restored.

Texas Beyond History: El Paso Missions

www.texasbeyondhistory.net/paso/kids.html

Find out more about what archaeologists have discovered from missions that once stood in El Paso.

Places to Visit

The Bob Bullock Texas State History Museum

1800 North Congress Avenue
Austin, TX 78701
(512) 936-8746
www.thestoryoftexas.com

See items that have been found at Texas missions, and view paintings of the missions.

San Antonio Missions National Historical Park

2202 Roosevelt Avenue
San Antonio, TX 78210
(210) 932-1001
www.nps.gov/saan

Tour the museum at the Alamo, and see Mission Concepción and Mission San José's famous Rose Window.

Important Words

acequia (ah-SEH-kee-uh) – a system of canals that carry water from a river to distant fields

adobe (uh-DOH-bee) – a building material of clay mixed with straw that is dried in the sun and made into bricks

archaeologists (ar-kee-AH-luh-jists) – scientists who study what is left behind by people of the past

bastions (BAS-chunz) – high corners of a fort from which cannons can be fired

convert – to cause to accept different ideas or beliefs

natural resources – materials that are found in nature and can be used by people in many ways

padres (PAH-drayz) – priests from Spanish-speaking countries

population – the total number of people living in an area

presidios (preh-SEE-dee-ohz) – forts built by the Spanish to protect missions

Index

Page numbers in **bold** indicate illustrations

About the Author

Megan Gendell has written and edited children's books about outer space, spies, magic tricks, and dinosaurs. She is a former editor at Scholastic and a graduate of Columbia University.